Duck Keeping

Beginner's Guide to Successfully Raising and Keeping Ducks (Choosing the Right Breed, Feeding, Breeding, Care...)

By Kenton Swinson

licensed professional before attempting any techniques outlined in this book.

By reading this document, the reader agrees that under no circumstances is the author responsible for any losses, direct or indirect, which are incurred as a result of the use of information contained within this document, including, but not limited to, —errors, omissions, or inaccuracies.

Contents

Thank you for buying this book and I hope that you will find it useful. If you will want to share your thoughts on this book, you can do so by leaving a review on the Amazon page, it helps me out a lot.

Introduction

Throughout the first weeks in which ducklings enter the world, they look so adorable, and individuals can't stand not to take a look at them. In the start, they do not do anything other than eating, pooping, and sleeping similar to human babies.

As they age, their feathers begin to show up, and they do not appear like the cute darlings that initially arrived on the scene. They grow really rapidly and within a couple of weeks, it's time for them to get bigger housing.

Considering that a duck is extremely fragile, they are not to be thrown around like a rock. They can not be pressed to the side even if you do not feel like hanging out with them. If that holds true, then do not get a duck.

They can not be sent in the wilderness where they can stroll free. Domestic ducks are raised captive and have been for a long period of time. For that reason, they can not fly since their legs are not sufficiently powerful.

They can't fly to food somewhere else when food for the winter season is not obtainable. If they do not have anybody to look after them, they are not going to make it through. Some individuals who do not understand what they're doing are going to feed them the incorrect foods, like chocolate and nuts . Doing this is going to aid them leave this planet faster.

If you have kids, it could be a tricky situation to look after ducks too. In case you are able to, have the ducks and kids separated. Also, raising ducks and kids is taxing.

You might wish to wait up until the kids can take care of themselves and you can give more time to the ducks. By that time, the kids are going to have the ability to help you with looking after them.

In case you have a cat or a dog, it may not be an excellent idea to have a duck. They both see ducks as food. They are not really delighted about a tame animal being in your house. They sense that the duck is a hazard attempting to invade their area. So you are going to need to decide regarding what you wish to do.

Considering that ducks need attention, you must not attempt to raise a duck if you won't give them the care and time that they require. It's not like searching for a babysitter for your kids, which can additionally be hard. Having somebody looking after your duck is not a thing that many individuals would want to do.

Make certain that you are going to have the ability to afford to pay veterinarian costs when your duck requires medical treatment. Ducks are seen as unique, so you are going to need to take them to a special veterinarian that focuses on exotic animals. Due to the specialty, it is going to cost you more for medical treatment and maintenance. In case you can't pay for it, then do not get a duck.

Individuals need to keep in mind that ducks are special animals which can not be left anyplace.

Numerous ducks are ditched every year since individuals realize that it's challenging to look after them. Yes, they are harder to look after than cats and dogs.

There are a lot of things that you need to carry out in order to keep them growing and healthy. The ideal thing to do is to learn about the appropriate duck care prior to you choosing to get one or more.

Chapter 1: Breed Selection

For novice duck owners, it can not be emphasized enough to make certain that you are prepared to raise and look after a duck or a great deal of them.

Selecting a breed is going to depend upon the purpose that you desire the duck for. If you desire a pet, you need to understand that some breeds are not going to connect with people. They prefer to be with their own.

The ideal breed of duck that would engage with people is the Pekin duck. They fancy humans and they are friendly. They additionally love to play and they are really warm towards others. This duck breeds would be one of the ideal sorts to raise.

If you are searching for one to display, there are certain ones that have gorgeous colors. The Cayuga is beautiful with its green color. The Khaki Campbell has a bronze color. Either of those breeds could make a home feel ornamental and warm.

If you desire eggs from the ducks, think of the runner duck breed. They can deliver the ideal eggs amongst the domestic ducks. They are simple to find and a few of them are fantastic as pets. If you have the ability to engage, spend time and appropriately look after them, they could be a terrific addition to your household.

Chapter 2: Duck Breeds

When you are raising and breeding ducks, it is necessary to understand what sort of breed you are dealing with. Every breed is distinct and has its own personality. There are lots of duck breeds, and a few of them are going to be gone over here.

Call Duck Breed-- This breed is utilized for decorative purposes. This duck is tinier than the majority of the other breeds.

Cayuga Duck Breed-- This duck is of a black color, yet, it does have a bit of green in it. It is an American breed of ducks and they are bigger than the Call Ducks. The females weigh approximately 6 pounds and the males weigh approximately 7.

Crested Duck Breed-- They originate from a mix of 2 other breeds of ducks, Aylesbury and Pekin duck breeds. Similar to call duck, the crested duck breed is utilized for decorative functions. On their heads, you are going to notice feather tufts.

Khaki Campbell Duck Breed-- This is an English breed of ducks and they are among the breeds that benefit raising ducks for eggs. These ducks generate approximately 400 duck eggs each year. Nevertheless, because they are light, they are not suggested for meat. They are additionally decorative in nature.

Muscovy Duck-- This breed of ducks is considered to be unappealing. It has feathers that are a mix of white and grey, while their crest is red and pink. You can additionally discover this duck in additional colors, like purple and blue. The female ducks can weigh approximately 12 pounds, while the male ones can weigh as much as 16 pounds. This is a breed which isn't recognized for swimming.

Buff Duck-- This is an English breed of ducks that is utilized for decorative purposes. Both males and females can weigh approximately around 9 pounds.

Pekin Duck-- This breed is the most prominent one in the United States. These ducks are great for making great meat. As far as egg laying is involved, they are not suggested for that. The female Pekin can weigh as much as 9 pounds, while the male one can weigh as much as 10 pounds.

Pomeranian Duck-- This is not an incredibly popular breed, and it is seldom seen. You will not discover a lot of breeders for this one, and they might end up being extinct.

Rouen Duck-- This breed resembles the Mallard duck, and some individuals are going to get them puzzled with the former. This is an incredibly popular breed, and for those who enjoy yard poultry, they enjoy the Rouen duck. They are great for the meat market. They are among the more simpler breeds to raise and have the ability to look after themselves.

Runner Duck-- This breed is recognized for being great egg layers. Nevertheless, this is one which the meat market would not desire. They are prominent, and individuals do utilize them for egg laying. Males and females can weigh approximately 4 pounds.

Chapter 3: Purchasing Ducks

You might be trying to find out where you can purchase a duck. There are numerous locations where ducks are offered. Some individuals believe that due to the fact that a duck could be seen as a pet, you can quickly get them at pet shops.

You can do that, but a pet shop is not the ideal location to acquire one. Some shops do not get the gender of the duck right, or if the shop has a lot of them, a few of them wind up getting ill or contracting an illness. You can additionally obtain them from online retailers or farms.

Wherever you obtain them from, make certain that it is a trustworthy place for selling ducks. You'll wish to check them out initially. If they have a site, then go to see what they offer. Read their warranties and policies. Remember that the more you buy, the lower the prices are going to be for every one. They generally post a bulk price to lure you into buying more.

You wish to go to a retailer that understands what they offer, and they ought to additionally have images of the ducks on their website so you can at least see what they appear like. It's more recommended to buy from a website that understands what the gender of their ducks is. You do not wish to buy one that you might believe is a male, yet it winds up being a female.

If you choose to buy on the web, you can get the animals shipped to your home. You can additionally attempt eBay and additional online retailers that offer ducks.

Chapter 4: Duck Fundamentals

In order to effectively look after your ducks, you are going to require fundamental basics. This is going to make sure that the ducks are going to be healthy.

In order to water and feed your ducks, you are going to require tools particularly produced for them. You can utilize waters and chicken feeders that are utilized for chickens. If you have a great deal of ducks, these products are going to be very valuable.

In case you have baby ducks, make sure the waterer is on a special stand. Or else, the young ones might make of mess of the waterer, making the litter become wet, which would transform it into the mold.

In the beginning, you may have the baby ducks in a little kennel. In case you have at minimum 10 of the young ones, have an allowance of 5 square feet. You are going to need to include more area for them to be home as they keep on aging and growing. Get something that is durable and is going to shield them from becoming wet. For the older ducks, they could be on the pasture.

When you own young ducks, make certain that they remain dry and comfy with litter created from the straw. They have to remain dry so that they will not need to handle mold, which can damage them. You'll wish to change their litter either daily or when it has to be changed.

Ducks have to drink and eat much like people. Supply them with a waterer so that they can put their head in the water. There should be enough water for them to do that. They could be fed chicken feed. Put the food in a hanging tube feeder. This could aid them not to squander the food so they may have a bit for the following time.

If it is truly cold, adult ducks are going to require heat. Baby ducks are going to require heat as they are still young. You may obtain a brooding light with a 250-watt bulb for the young ones. As they grow and get more feathers, they will not require that amount of heat.

Chapter 5: Nesting And Hatching

If you choose to get your ducks from the ground up (a mom duck), there are certain things that you want to learn about the nesting and hatching procedure.

Do not get anxious when your ducks are nesting or are about to lay eggs. The mom duck is going to do most of the work. You simply want to understand what to anticipate with the procedure. Ultimately, you are going to master whatever you have to do.

If you do not intend to keep all of the ducklings that the mom duck has, they must not all be hatched. As the mom duck lays the eggs, you may get rid of them. Nevertheless, if you do have space and the cash to look after them, then, of course, you may do so.

The ideal location to do that is on a farm or someplace where you have a great deal of area. If you live among others, you'll most likely need to contact your local government to check if you are even able to look after ducks.

As far as nesting is regarded, the mom duck ought to be housed in a safe location, far from other animals. A complete nest is considered to be 12 eggs. She is going to most likely desire soft bed linen, such as hay, to rest on in addition to the eggs. Do not construct a nest since she will not utilize it. While she is nesting, everybody else ought to be kept away, specifically kids.

The hatching procedure needs a minimum of thirty days for all of the eggs to come out. When the procedure begins, the initial ones hatch within a day. In case there are eggs that are vigorously pressed out of the nest, they are no longer alive. The mom understands this and presses those eggs far from the other ones. If there are split or cracked eggs, there might be a disturbance with the nest.

If the mom is nesting, she ought to be left alone. She does not like being troubled when she's at that phase. She can get upset and irritable. Additionally, she might reveal an aggressive side that you might be sorry for later on. Although they understand who you are by now, they still do not wish to be troubled. In case they see anybody that they do not recognize, she might leave the nest.

If she is not near water, supply a reservoir with water. She ought to additionally have food, however, do not leave it out for an extended period of time. Do not leave it out overnight, however. There is a considerable risk of bugs and other unwanted visitors that can visit.

To keep her food from being interrupted, you can put a couple of worms or a bit of food beside the water and leave it there for a couple of hours.

There might be times when the mom is going to leave the nest:

- She went to get food and water for nutrition.

- She got frightened about something and deserted the nest. Offer her a couple of days to come back; if not, then get rid of the eggs.

- The weather condition is too cold or too hot.

- The incubation procedure can move on without her due to the warm weather condition.

- In case the mom can't hatch eggs, they are going to choose to quit and abandon the nest.

Remember that all eggs from the mom might not hatch. Those that have not hatched ought to be done away with after 2 days. Take them out thoroughly so that they do not break.

The dad duck ought to be separated from the baby ducks and the mom right away. Given the captivity aspect and the fact that the family is bigger now, it's feasible that the male duck can injure or kill the kids.

The mom duck ought to be permitted to spend time with ducklings. They are going to keep warm and she could teach them a couple of things. Give it a week, and after that, position the ducklings in a brooder.

Chapter 6: Looking After Ducklings

Taking care of ducks is not a tough task. When you are enthusiastic, you are going to do an excellent job. As you see them grow, they are going to develop into adult ducks ultimately. You should ensure that they are looked after and raised appropriately.

Baby ducks are going to reside in a brooding location. You can pick a little facility or home them in the barn corner. It is essential that they are safeguarded, so the brooding location needs to be confined. They need to be shielded against animals that might hurt or perhaps kill them.

Animals that would fit the mold are raccoons, foxes, cats and dogs. Considering that the ducks are so little, they are helpless and have to be kept away from the bigger animals. In order to shut out bacteria, the brooding location needs to remain tidy, dry, lighted and constantly aerated.

The ducks need to have good bed linen in their living quarters. You can utilize hay or straw for the bed linen. Do not utilize wood shavings or chips due to the fact that the little ducks might end up being ill. Change their bed linen daily, particularly if it's musty or wet.

To supply them with sufficient heat, utilize a heat light with an infrared bulb. Usually, routine light bulbs do not offer ample heat from them. The number of ducklings you are looking after is going to determine the wattage that you are going to require.

For the first 10 days when the ducks are home, keep the temperature level at 99 Fahrenheit. The temperature level is going to go down by 5 Fahrenheit weekly as you raise the lamp. Keep at this until the temperature level reaches 70 Fahrenheit. It could take up to a month and a half to reach this temperature level.

Do not make it possible for direct light to get in contact with the ducklings. Put the heat far from them. You are going to recognize if they are comfortable with the temperature level if they are active and they drink and eat. They are going to be uneasy in case they go away from the heat. You are going to understand that they are too cold if they make a great deal of noise and congregate in a group.

Ducklings have to have a duck starter as you're feeding them. This is a tool that assists you in feeding the duck. A few of the very best foods for them are carefully sliced vegetables and fruits. They need to consume food that can go down quickly due to the fact that they do not have teeth.

They can additionally consume worms and other little bugs. What they can not eat are dry bread, onions, birdseed and grains. The bread is specifically hazardous since it can mold, and the ducklings can pass away if they eat that.

Chapter 7: Looking After Adult Ducks

Ducks grow rapidly, and soon, they are going to become grownups. Even as they age, they still have to be looked after like the ducklings. They are still growing and are going to have to be nurtured.

The feeder ought to be dry and tidy. If there are any sharp locations of the feeder, utilize duct tape to cover them up. Store the feeder in a safe location within their dwelling area.

They ought to eat pellet food which contains ample protein. In case they are laying eggs, they ought to consume no more than 20 percent in their food. In case they aren't laying eggs, the optimum quantity ought to be 17 percent.

It's harmful to offer older ducks large quantities of protein since it can impact their wings. Angel wing is a condition due to which their wings stay up. In other case, if they do not get an ample quantity of protein, they are not going to have the ability to lay eggs effectively.

Older ducks can consume green veggies. Enable them to consume weeds and grass if they live outdoors. Veggies or at least green veggies ought to constantly be part of their day-to-day diet plan. You can additionally feed them hard-boiled eggs.

The eggs ought to be sliced up. In addition to that, they can eat little bugs, consisting of worms. Any treats that the ducks get ought to be allocated to weekly portions. You can not let the ducks overindulge, or they may pass away.

Do not feed them entire corn due to the fact that it might mess with their gastrointestinal system. They can consume split corn. Split corn is more helpful for them throughout the winter. Split corn has a fair bit of protein.

Ensure that the older ducks have water. It assists with digestion, and the water could be utilized by them to clean their beaks. They ought to constantly have water or, otherwise, they might choke during eating. Change their water daily.

The food must never ever be out of date and stagnant. Do not leave food within the feeder. It can rapidly contract bacteria. Switch out the food in the event that the ducks are not eating it in a reasonable manner.

Ensure that the feeder constantly has food that is great for their health. Do not offer them seeds, or it might mess with their gastrointestinal system. They are going to not get anything good from consuming food that people eat. Avoid giving them chocolate. Chocolate is bad for them, and they might pass away if they eat it.

Chapter 8: Duck Maintenance

Ducks that live domestically do not need wing clipping. Nevertheless, in case they do, the feathers have to be clipped appropriately, or otherwise, they might be hurt, get an infection and bleed to death. In case the wings have to be clipped, take them to a veterinarian for expert treatment.

Ducks can get hurt. Something that can stop this is you supplying them with ample space so that they can walk around.

Ducks undergo a phase called molting. Approximately every 6 months, they are going to begin to lose a great deal of feathers. Throughout the regrowing procedure, the wings are going to be delicate. Stay clear of touching their wings up until they have actually grown back.

Ducks protect their legs by having a broad ramp to ensure that they can get in and out of the water securely. Additionally, it is not a great idea to place them in a wire cage since that can induce harm too. If the duck's toes or feet ache, that ought to concern you. Contact a veterinarian and have the duck looked at.

Stop your duck from being subjected to harmful things or locations. Copper, zinc and lead are the things that ducks come across the most. Nails, chemicals, pesticides, screws, coins, and other little things can be harmful when they come in contact with the ducks. If you see it sufficiently early, the veterinarian is able to administer treatment.

The veterinarian would administer laxatives and injections to eliminate the infection. Please do not attempt to treat your duck personally. This is a really major matter and must not be ignored.

There are several additional foods that ducks must not consume. They can induce damage to their bodies. Any type of seeds, nuts or chocolate must not be offered to them. It might make them ill, and they may potentially pass away.

Do not give your duck too much protein. An excessive amount of it can result in them establishing "Slipped Wing" or "Angel Wing." This is a condition during which the primary feathers aren't growing properly due to extreme protein in their system. Decrease the protein levels that you are offering them. The duck's wings are going to grow back usually.

Mating Problems-- You are going to know when the female and male ducks are mating due to the fact that the female ducks are going to have spots on their neck or head. You might additionally notice these spots around the eyes.

Additionally, you might notice a crust atop the female's head that originates from the male spewing mucous. Ensure that you have tidy water so they can swim in it. Without it, they are going to run the risk of infection and injury because of uneasy breeding.

Beak discolorations or spots – In case your duck reveals indications of stainings on their beak, call your veterinarian. There is no cause that has actually been established regarding why that takes place. Nevertheless, it ought to still be enough of a reason to see a vet.

In case you notice bumps on the duck's beak, it generally originates from them digging or pecking. In case the bump is like a blister, have the veterinarian drain the fluid and apply lotion to do away with the germs. Get rid of any sharp surface areas close to the duck.

Breathing Issues – In case you duck has the signs of a cold, call your veterinarian right away. They could catch pneumonia in a change of weather condition. If they are subjected to water or cool air for an extended amount of time, they can get a cold or similar disease.

They ought to remain warm and dry after they have actually gone swimming. If you believe that they might have a pneumonia or cold, call your veterinarian or an alternative veterinarian instantly. The faster your duck gets treatment, the faster they can recuperate.

In order for your duck to remain healthy, the environment has to always be tidy and devoid of anything that might hurt them or make them ill. Keep pesticides and chemicals hidden. Any bins that are utilized for water and food ought to be tidy and without bugs.

For young ducks, change their linen two times a day; for adult ones, you may change it daily. If you wish to go green, duck droppings could be utilized as fertilizer for veggies and plants.

Ducks resemble people in many ways. They have to be taken care of, so make certain to supply them with love. They can additionally experience depression and feel lonesome when you overlook them. Spend some time having fun with them. They enjoy balls, stuffed animals and toys that drift in the water. It's incredible how they get in touch with the human experience.

Chapter 9: Duck Conditions

Maggots-- When the ducks do not have an ample water supply to remain tidy, they can bring in maggots. If the vent is unclean, that is partially why the ducks get struck with this illness. The maggots could be eliminated by utilizing fly spray and an ointment.

You should keep your eye on ducks for numerous days consecutively. In case they currently have fly eggs, they are still going to hatch.

Mites-- When the ducks are scratching exceedingly, it might be an indication of mites. Other birds with mites could send them to the ones that are healthy. In case you have chickens and ducks together, there is a higher likelihood of the ducks getting mites.

The mites are going to collect on the duck's wings and the plumes are going to turn gray in color. To get rid of them, you are going to need to utilize a pesticide. You can additionally utilize flea spray to eliminate the mites.

Treat the ducks with this for approximately least 4 days. To stop another round of mites, dust powder in the locations where mites gather, in open cracks and nesting locations.

Botulism-- When ducks have this illness, they are unable to swallow a thing. Plus, they have actually lost control of their muscles in their neck, legs, and wings. If ducks are close to locations where there is veggie and/or animal waste, they might come in contact with toxic substances that originate from germs.

For treatment, they can consume fresh drinking water. Considering that they can't swallow, you might need to give it to them utilizing a tube. You can additionally include Epsom salt in the drinking water. So as to avoid a recurrence, the ducks must not remain in locations that are muddy and unclean.

It the weather condition is hot, it's much more important for them to stay away from unclean and muddy water, and also from water that has been stagnant for some time. When the ducks remain in a hot temperature area, the germs collect rapidly.

Lead poison-- The signs of lead poisoning in ducks consist of very little coordination and weight loss. The poison can originate from paint that is lead-based. So. to avoid a recurrence, keep them far from paint and permit them to have the grit to make sure they are not in contact with lead.

Breathing problems-- The duck has a challenging time breathing, so their tail is going to go down and up so that they could obtain some air. They are additionally in a hunched-up position. In case the weather condition is wet, the ducks may get a bacterial infection. To eliminate this, provide the ducks with an antibiotic.

Angel Wing or Slipped Wing-- You are going to understand that your duck is impacted by this illness if their wings turn outwards. This is brought on by the duck consuming excessive protein.

This induces them to grow faster than anticipated. The wings become heavy due to too much blood in the quills. The treatment for this is to provide less protein as they are trying to grow their main feathers.

Sinus-- When ducks have sinus, their cheeks are going to get puffy and swell. Additionally, their nostrils are going to be runny. Ducks can catch sinus from germs that are drifting in the air. The treatment for this could be via antibiotics.

It needs to begin immediately in order for the recovery to work. The veterinarian is going to need to flush the sinuses with antibiotics up until the swelling decreases. Do not postpone treatment as the duck's cheeks are going to get hard, and the treatment is not going to work after that. Hardening of the cheeks can not be reversed.

Pasteurella-- The ducks are not going to be hungry. They are going to be thirstier and are going to produce droppings that are green in color. They are not going to have coordination. This illness originates from germs in the air. Fast treatment that includes antibiotics needs to be given to ducks. Eliminate any carriers of this illness.

Coccidiosis-- This illness strikes the stomach lining. The signs of this illness consist of droppings blended with blood. When the stomach lining is struck, the ducks can not take in and digest nutrients from the food they eat.

This illness might wreck them for numerous weeks. To treat this, pour anticoccidial in the drinking water. Although this is an uncommon illness for ducks, it's great to learn about it so that you understand what to do in case they get it. Ideally, they are never going to.

Enteritis-- The ducks are going to produce droppings that are pink. They are going to feel listless and will not have the energy to move like they wish to. This normally takes place in the summer season when they have hot spells.

This leads to them getting germs in their stomach, which can induce irritation in the stomach. They might additionally experience bleeding in that location. The veterinarian can provide the duck with a vaccine. They need to get the vaccine right away.

They can additionally get antibiotics to deal with the illness. It is thought that this illness originates from wild birds. Keep the ducks in a tidy location for a couple of days.

Lameness - The duck's hock or ankle are going to be inflamed. Their legs are going to feel hot. This illness can originate from an infection because of germs. For treatment, the veterinarian is going to administer injections with antibiotics.

Even if you understand what illness your ducks are dealing with, it's still advised to take them to the veterinarian for verification and extra treatment.

Chapter 10: Duck Behavior

At the 4 week mark, ducks are going to incubate their eggs. There is a 24-hour duration when the eggs hatch. The infant ducks that are born need to have a location to cohabitate. Wild and domestic ducks do not mix.

Ducks are not created to be potty trained. Often they let it out prior to getting to that location where they can dispose of it. As you monitor them, you can notice a pattern. Based on what they do and when, you are going to have the ability to identify when they let it out and put them inside when the time is right. If you desire, you can utilize non-reusable diapers (preemies), diaper harness or baggies.

When it comes to wild ducks, they could be free to do what they desire. With domestic ducks, they don't quite have that freedom. They need to discover how to live a rather restricted life. They can move around, however, it's on a tinier scale than what you would observe with wild ones. Domestic ducks depend upon people to look after them.

The male ducks can, in some cases, become aggressive at 6 months or older. They like to go after other ducks and pinch. You can't let this intensify; otherwise, it is going to get challenging to stop them as time passes.

You should persist in order to help alter their aggressive behavior. Something you may do to get them to quit pinching you is to carefully tap your fingernail on the beak while saying "no." You need to be strong and stern, yet calm.

Given that ducks are so tender, you need to be cautious about the way you manage them. Do not be physically harsh with them. Some individuals have actually claimed to hold their beak to get them to act correctly. Nevertheless, that might not be a great idea considering that they need to get air. As soon as you develop that trust with your duck(s), they are going to discover that aggressive conduct is not how it should be.

You can get them a mate or offer them a location big enough where they are able to run around. Make certain to show your duck(s) a lot of love. It can take some time before they choose to bond with you.

Another method to develop trust is to spend some quiet time with them, or to feed them from your hand. They are going to begin to recognize that you truly do take care of them.

Do not let young kids manage the ducks by themselves. Either the kid or the duck could be hurt because of rough play or something comparable.

Chapter 11: Looking After Ducks In All Sorts Of Weather

Throughout the winter, ducks require ventilation along with ample heat. A infrared or ceramic bulb or a 75-100 watt basic bulb could be utilized depending upon the environment that you live in. If you are utilizing bulbs for heat, have them at a height at which the ducks can't get to them.

Put them in a location where the ducks can go to another location in case the light becomes too hot. Additionally, keep it far from combustible things.

For harsh weather conditions, develop a shelter that has a roof that is water-resistant, an entry-exit door with a rubber flap and insulated walls that can withstand wind. The ducks are going to be shielded from severe weather conditions in addition to having the ability to go outside.

Other options consist of utilizing a basement during nights or a garage. They ought to have ample water and food and ensure that it is sufficiently warm for them to remain there.

When it comes to the cold winter season weather, certain domestic ducks can handle it more than others. If it is truly cold, they are going to get close and develop a huddle so as to remain warm. Ducks have to remain warm in very cold temperature levels, particularly if they fluctuate all of a sudden.

Otherwise, they can get ill. The shelter ought to be tidy while keeping it dry. If the shelter is not dry, the duck(s) can get infected. Do not let mold or anything that is a hazard to them to grow in their shelter.

You can utilize rubber sheds to house them during the evening. Drill holes to ensure that there is ventilation. You ought to have a strategy in place to develop the shelter before the winter. When it comes, you simply need to make a fast shift.

Have an aerator or a pump available to keep little ponds thawed out. Or you can head to a store that sells items for de-icing ponds, like a pond heating unit. When the pond is thawed, harmful gasses leave and oxygen arrives. Regardless of that, the ideal thing to utilize is the pond heating unit.

Throughout the summertime season, ducks do not require a great deal of shelter. Nevertheless, they must not be subjected to the sun a lot. Like people, they can get sunstroke if they remain in the sun too much. They ought to have fresh water to consume, shade and shelter.

Chapter 12: Tips On How To Protect Against Duck Illness

Make certain that what they're consuming is nutritional. Ducks ought to constantly have fresh drinking water. If the water does not appear like it's safe to drink, toss it out and substitute it with water that is tidy, fresh and cool for them to take in. The container which it is housed in ought to be washed at least once every day.

Supply ducks with a wholesome meal. The food ought to be portioned well; otherwise, the ducks may get an illness.

The troughs need to be dry and tidy constantly. In case the trough is wet, there is a higher likelihood that it could be infested with mold and germs.

If you have ducks that are the identical age, have them together in the identical dwelling and provide the identical medication to every one of them.

The location where the ducks wander and gather ought to constantly be tidy with dry litter and correctly drained, so it remains dry.

The location where the ducks sleep during the night ought to be shielded from animals that are larger than them, like cats, dogs and big rodents. They can quickly transmit various kinds of illness.

Ducks must not be included in a great deal of action since they can get stressed out. They would not have the ability to produce as much.

The location in which the ducks are housed ought to have a lot of ventilation. Do not crowd the dwelling up. The ducks are going to still require space to walk around.

So as to keep them healthy, offer your ducks a vitamin-mineral supplement which has antibiotics.

Don't feed the ducks with fish, dead snails and meat that might be ruined. It may be poisonous and damaging to ducks.

In case you give rice to the ducks, make certain it does not have any damaging chemicals, like insecticides.

Spray the ducks at least once per year to keep away mice, beetles and anything else that might be bad for them.

If you get brand-new ducks, keep them far from the other ducks for a minimum of two weeks. You do not wish your present brood to catch any illness from blending with the brand-new ducks.

Put footbaths in various areas. This can assist in protecting your property against foreign agents.

Conclusion

In conclusion, ducks can make excellent pets, however, you need to have the willingness to invest the time it is going to require to raise and support them in the appropriate manner. They require a lot of attention and if you are unable to provide what they require, then you must not have them as a pet.

In the very first couple of weeks, they are extremely fragile animals, and after that, they mature into a buddy for people. There are individuals who like to have ducks as pets and there are some individuals who believe that they are crazy for doing that.

There is a great deal of work associated with raising ducks. You need to be prepared and get yourself ready for the experiences you are going to have with these animals.

I hope that you enjoyed reading through this book and that you have found it useful. If you want to share your thoughts on this book, you can do so by leaving a review on the Amazon page. Have a great rest of the day.

Printed in Great Britain
by Amazon